Stand with Children

A movement founded by
Catholics for the Common Good Institute

Mission Statement

Promote the reality that marriage unites a man and a woman with each other and any children born from their union.

Stand with the common interest that each and therefore every child without exception has in knowing and being cared for, as far as possible, by his or her mother and father preferably united in marriage.

Promote the recognition of this interest by laws, societal institutions, and individuals.

standwithchildren.org
P.O. Box 320038
San Francisco, CA 94132
415-651-4171
info@ccgaction.org

Emmaus Road Publishing
827 North Fourth Street
Steubenville, Ohio 43952

© 2012 Catholics for the Common Good Institute
All rights reserved. Published 2012
Printed in the United States of America
15 14 13 12 1 2 3 4 5

Library of Congress Control Number: 2012942899
ISBN: 978-1-937155-80-3

Cover design and layout by
Theresa Westling

Dedication

The *Stand with Children* movement is dedicated to Our Lady of Guadalupe, our role model and guide for the inculturation of faith and evangelization of culture, and to Blessed John Paul II, who continues to teach us about marriage and family every day.

We ask their intercession for the restoration of a culture that promotes men and women marrying before having children and supports them in their marriage.

TABLE OF CONTENTS

Appendix:

PART 1
Rebuilding a Marriage Culture

Have you ever been in a discussion about marriage and not known how to explain it in non-religious terms? Have you ever had conversations around the Thanksgiving dinner table with extended family members and heard all kinds of opinions about the purpose of marriage and who should be allowed to marry? If you have children or grandchildren, have you struggled to answer the tough questions that they bring home from school? Have you ever had difficulty explaining the difference between civil and religious marriage or why the government should be in the business of sanctioning marriages at all? Perhaps you too have some unanswered questions about marriage.

Today, we are in the middle of a public policy debate about what marriage is and why it is important. The fact that there is even a debate about policy is evidence of cultural confusion about what marriage is. That confusion has dire consequences for every family and the whole of society.

While it is the dream of every parent to see their children grow up and continue their family built on the foundation of a happy marriage, this is happening less and less today. The percentage of high school seniors who aspire to marriage has remained unchanged over the years, but the number achieving their dreams has dropped precipitously. As a result, today over four of ten children in America are being born to unmarried mothers. Marriage is in crisis.

While many blame the current controversy over the purpose and societal benefits of marriage on the gay rights movement, the roots of the problem are much deeper and more serious. Marriage is in crisis because it has become nothing more than an adult centric institution, no longer the foundation of the family, in the minds of an increasing number of people. Protecting the traditional definition of marriage in the law is critical to prevent the elimination of the only institution that unites kids with their moms and dads, but defending the status quo is not enough. Dealing with the problem at it roots and working to rebuild a culture that encourages men and women to marriage before having children must become an imperative of social justice. Every family has a stake in this.

Searching for Clearer Ways to Communicate

In 2007, Catholics for the Common Good started looking for new ways to understand and communicate the reality of marriage in collaboration with the California Catholic Conference (of Bishops). Legislation redefining marriage and the family had been flying through the state legislature, and those trying to witness the truth about these institutions were struggling to make credible arguments without appearing to be "anti-gay." We know what marriage is down deep. We know what our faith teaches about it, but how to express what we know to be true and cannot be any other way is challenging in this culture.

We started to look at marriage and family from the perspective of children and the common interest that each and all without exception have in the marriage of their moms and dads. The *Stand with Children* movement for the evangelization of culture on marriage and family was born.

The following year we put the project on hold when the California Catholic Conference asked us to lead the lay Catholic part of the Proposition 8 campaign. In May of that year, the California Supreme Court found it discriminatory to deny same-sex couples the right to participate in marriage and overturned the state's marriage protection law adopted by the voters in 2000. The Prop 8 victory in November 2008 restored the traditional definition of marriage by placing it in the state constitution, out of the reach of the state courts. All the victory did, however, was to permit a continued debate about what marriage is in California and open the door to more lawsuits at the Federal level.

After the campaign we continued to work with the volunteer leadership team we assembled, and held trainings, workshops and seminars about how to communicate the reality of marriage to family and friends. The formation materials were based on Catholic social teaching, and particularly the teaching of Blessed John Paul II on marriage, the family and the human person. We found the teaching translated rather easily into non-religious language that is easy for anyone to understand. These workshops became laboratories of learning and spiritual formation, leading us to a deeper understanding about methods and challenges of communicating the reality of love, marriage, family, and human sexuality in this age of relativism.

What became clear to us was that in our relativistic culture where most of us tend to make decisions based on our own point of view (i.e., "what is true for you may not be true for me"), we are tempted to reject objective truth or Catholic teaching as unreasonable if it does not conform to our experience. However, the more deeply we understand Catholic social teaching and become able to apply and communicate its principles in non-religious language, to the great surprise of many, it becomes stunningly reasonable, even to non-believers. The challenge is in its communication.

Working with high school students in the 1950s, an Italian priest, Luigi Giussani, discovered that questioning youth, drawing on common human experience and reason while pursuing the Beautiful, the True and the Good, could verify the reality of their faith in ways that inspired them to go more deeply into the Mystery. It gave birth to the ecclesial movement, Communion and Liberation.[1] Many believe that Blessed John Paul II was so effective in communicating with young people because he had a way of teaching that resonated with the heart

---

1   Dwight Longenecker, *Risk of Faith* (New Haven: Catholic Information Service, Knights of Columbus, 2008).

and common human experience. He did not tell young people what they wanted to hear, but they knew what he told them exuded the truth, goodness and beauty of undeniable Reality. We need to learn and follow Blessed John Paul's example.

Reality-Based Thinking

Our adviser and board member, Father Michael Sweeney, O.P., President of the Dominican School of Philosophy and Theology in Berkeley, CA, reminded us, that the teaching of the Catholic Church does not create reality, but provides us with a deeper understanding of it. In other words, it is important to consider, that things are not simply true because they are in the Bible; they are in the Bible because they are, first and foremost, true. There are some things that we cannot know about God or ourselves without the benefit of divine revelation. However, there are many fundamental things we can know by turning to common human experience, reason and the pursuit of beauty and goodness. In fact the search itself reveals certain truths about ourselves that are valuable in our quest for true love, true freedom and true happiness.

For example, when we look at marriage through the eyes of the child, we become like a child[2] and we begin to see the reality of what marriage is. Putting ourselves in the place of the child, marriage is no longer an abstraction, it is a reality. We can recall our own desire for knowing our origins and being loved and

---

2   Matthew 18:3.

cared for by our mother and father. Even if we never knew our mother and father or by some circumstances felt alienated from them, that desire is still there. Contemplating this, the reality of marriage in God's plan for creation becomes apparent to all, but is not dependent on belief in God. It is a fact stamped right into our very nature.

In a time when children are created to fulfill the desires of adults through assisted reproductive technology (ART), it is sometimes easy to forget that every child without exception has a mother and a father. However, they do. It is a fact. The loss of one or both is a real privation of something that is common to each and therefore all, and is good (meaning that which contributes to human flourishing or development). Indeed, a mother and father, our brothers and sisters and extended family are part of who we are. It is a tragedy when children are deprived of their families due to circumstances beyond anyone's control, but especially when it is done intentionally without just cause. This is an example of what Catholics for the Common Good calls "reality-based thinking."

From our post Prop 8 workshops with committed marriage advocates, we also learned that we are all products of our culture and can unwittingly accept false premises as true. As a very orthodox Catholic deacon from Bakersfield observed, "I am starting to realize that sometimes I say things that conflict with what I believe." We all do. Sometimes we try to use reasoning to make a point starting with something that is untrue without realizing it, such as: "The most important thing to a child is to have someone who loves them" or "He or she has a right to a child to be fulfilled," etc. Parts 4, 5 and 6 (Frequently Asked Questions) address these false premises by using reality-based thinking and grounding the content in indisputable reality that can be verified with common human experience and reason.

Focusing on reality can be shocking at times because it is counter cultural or conflicts with political correctness. Sometimes uncomfortable questions cannot be avoided. In the film, *Hear No Evil, See No Evil,* the comedian Richard Pryor played a blind concession stand worker. When his sister alluded to his experience as a black man, he reacted with wide eyes, feeling his face, and exclaiming, "What? You mean I'm not white? Does mom know?" It was a very funny scene because it recognized the obvious.

So it is in the case of children who have been deprived of their mother or father or both, sometimes intentionally. Mom knows and so does the child, but no one dares say it. Some will swear that their children are not deprived of the fundamental human right or experience, and the donated sperm or egg the child emanated from was merely a disembodied cell. "Reality" in this case often is forced to conform to the interests of the adults, but *real* reality is evident to the child. Someone from whom they originated is missing. That is reality.

Instead, the culture promulgates that it is normative for a child to not have a mother or father and that it is OK. In fact, as you will learn in Part 3, almost a majority of young people believe it is good to have an increased number of family types (other than families with married mothers and fathers). When you consider the reality that children in alternative families by definition are deprived of their mothers and fathers united in marriage, it is mindboggling how anyone can claim this is a good thing. Yet this false assumption is being taught in schools and being embraced by many young people today. It is based on the cultural misconception that the right of adults to be fulfilled supersedes the fundamental human right of children. How can this be true?

As noted above, it is so easy for all of us to be lulled into accepting false realities and make mistakes as a result. As my college-age son tried to explain to me, it is OK for women to have children with sperm donors because in their "reality" they have no intention of depriving the child of his or her father. Their intention is only to be fulfilled by having a child that would never have otherwise existed. After quite a bit of discussion, he finally saw reality (from the perspective of the child) and understood that intention does not change reality. This is an example how we can make mistakes even with good intentions. When we become aware of them, it often evokes feelings of remorse or shame. It is not our place to judge, but to recognize our collective brokenness, and to love and promote healing. The work of evangelization of culture for marriage and family is about educating and forming ourselves based on Reality (which incidentally always points to Christ and the Trinity), and witnessing it with love by the way we live our lives. It is not about criticizing others for past mistakes.

Formation for Evangelization of Culture

As many of the participants discovered in our workshops, we must have the humility to recognize that we are all in need of learning and formation. Our focus must be on ourselves and solidarity with the victims of the breakdown of marriage—future children deprived of married mothers and fathers, and young people deprived of their dreams for marriage because of misconceptions about love, sexuality, and marriage. Focusing on people who are perceived adversaries harms us as it drains grace, obstructs our ability to love, and creates a false sense of righteousness in us. To avoid this temptation, it is useful to follow Christ's example on the Cross, "Father, forgive them; for they know not what they do."[3]

As Archbishop Charles Chaput told the Fellowship of Catholic Scholars in 2010, "[D]ismantling the inhuman parody we call 'modern American culture' begins not with violence but with the conversion of our own hearts. . . . Your task . . . is to strengthen that spirit in each other . . . and to instill it in all the people you reach with the extraordinary skills God has given you. If you do *only that*, but do it well, then God will do the rest."

---

3   Luke 23:34.

Faith and Action Circles

We all have different gifts given by God. Following Archbishop Chaput's advice for the evangelization of culture, we must focus on our own conversion and formation. As Pope Benedict XVI has said, it is important to create a sense of the "we" of the Church. We are not on this journey alone. We are like participants in a mountain climbing party, roped together with each other and with Christ, ascending the heights. Sometimes we need to help pull someone else along and sometimes we need a little tug.[4]

An increasing number of people are participating in *Stand with Children* by forming small groups of peers into Faith and Action Circles. Participants meet on a regular basis to read, reflect and gain insights to be shared with family and friends. These circles become support groups for finding practical solutions in dealing with cultural influences that undermine the understanding of true love, marriage and family with our children and family members.

Initially, participants of the Faith and Action Circles can start by reading and reflecting on this guide. Following that, additional content will be provided to support the ongoing formation for evangelizing the culture for marriage and family.

We hope this booklet will meet your immediate needs for insights on how to discuss marriage and family issues with friends and family members. We also hope the exposure to the content of the booklet, which is derived from Catholic social teaching, will help build confidence that the Church has the

---

4   Pope Benedict XVI, Palm Sunday homily, (March 28, 2010).

answers—we just need to know where to look for them and how to communicate them to the people we love.

There are reasons for hope. The current crisis in marriage as discussed in Part 3 must and can be reversed. However, it will take a massive educational effort and organization. It will take courageous men and women who are willing to speak up and advocate the truth about marriage and family when issues are on the ballot or before the legislature. We need to work for government policies that promote men and women marrying before having children.

But the discussion about the meaning of love, marriage, family and human sexuality is going on every day in classrooms, in work places, through television, movies and music. It is everywhere and it is influencing our children and friends. The discussion will go on with or without us. We hope that as you read this booklet, you will consider the consequences of not preparing to participate.

Remember, the real work of evangelizing the culture on marriage and family begins around the family dinner table. It is there that children must be inoculated against the influences of the culture by providing them with the verifiable truth about love, marriage, family and human sexuality.

After you have read this booklet, consider joining the *Stand with Children* movement and Catholics for the Common Good.

∞⌘∞

PART 2
Public Policy:
The Civil Recognition of Marriage

What is Marriage?

The question about public policy regarding marriage and proposals to redefine it to accommodate same-sex couples comes down to a decision between two conflicting understandings (definitions) of marriage:

1. Marriage is the public recognition of a committed relationship between a man and a woman (or two adults) for their fulfillment.

2. **Marriage unites a man and a woman with each other and *any* children born from their union.**

Which definition is *true*, and which definition serves the public interest?

The second definition is known as "traditional" marriage, but there is nothing traditional about it. It is a fact. Marriage unites a man and a woman with each other and any children born from their union. That is what marriage is, and that is what it does. It expresses God's plan for creation but is not dependent on belief in God. This human reality can only be recognized by states, cultures, and religions, but can never change. It is the same reality recognized by every society, every culture and every religion, each according to their own competencies.[1]

Many people, particularly our youth, view marriage as described in the first definition. As sex, child bearing, and child rearing have become increasingly disassociated with marriage over the last forty years, it is increasingly seen as solely adult-centric. Most consequential was "no-fault divorce," which effectively redefined marriage as only a committed relationship that is valid as long as both parties are happy. The great lie of "no-fault divorce" is, "If the adults are happy, the children will be happy." Increasingly, people have come to think of marriage as a means of pursuing individual happiness.

However, marriage is much more than an institution for adult fulfillment. Although attitudes have changed, the reality of marriage has not. Marriage between a man and a woman is still the only institution that unites kids with their moms and dads.

Explaining the Reality of Marriage

Memorize this phrase. **"Marriage unites a man and a woman with each other and *any* children born from their union."** It expresses the **fullness** of what marriage is; it is a complete response in secular language to the question of

---

1   For example, Catholics recognize the same reality of marriage as in civil marriage but with a deeper understanding of its beauty and significance. Between baptized persons we know that marriage is a sacrament and a source of supernatural grace. We understand it as a reflection of the inner life of the Trinity and the relationship between Christ and his Church. See Catechism of the Catholic Church (hereafter CCC) 1603.

"What is marriage?" It describes the communion of man and woman leading to a communion between parent and child, a "communion of persons."[2]

Marriage is greater than the sum of its parts. Its goods for the human person and society can be more easily recognized when described in this way. The phrase describes an intimate community of life and love, and expresses procreation, complementarity, motherhood and fatherhood, irreplaceability, non-substitutability, kinship, family, the good of children, *and even the potential for the heartbreak of infertility.* Its uniqueness as a societal institution is apparent.

Here is another way to describe marriage that reveals the truth about it, the human person and the family. In marriage, a man and a woman freely choose to make themselves irreplaceable to each other. Until that point, everyone is replaceable. It is through their marriage that they become irreplaceable to each other. This free choice for irreplaceability and a commitment to the common good of the unit is precisely what prepares them to receive the fruit of their union, a new person, as a gift of equal value and dignity to each of them.[3]

In reality, the man *and* woman are irreplaceable to their child, and their child is irreplaceable to the mother and father: it was the marriage that started that circle of irreplaceability that

---

2   Blessed Pope John Paul II, Apostolic Exhortation on the Role of Christian Family in the Modern World *Familiaris Consortio* (November 22, 1981), no. 21; *Letter to Families* (February 2, 1994), no. 7-8.

3   William E. May, *Marriage the Rock on Which the Family is Built* (Ignatius Press: San Francisco, 2009).

we call the family. That is what marriage is, and that is what it does. "Therefore a man leaves his father and his mother and cleaves to his wife, and they become one flesh" (Gen. 2:24). The child is an eternal witness to the union of the mother and father, carrying their flesh, and the mother and father and extended family are part of the child's identity.[4] This is reality. It is beautiful and good.

What is "same-sex marriage"?

When people come to understand marriage as only an institution for individual fulfillment and happiness, there is no longer any inherent connection between the relationship of the adults, procreation, children, and a family of common ancestry. Therefore the reason for marriage to be recognized only as a union of a man and a woman is no longer apparent.

The term "same-sex marriage" gives the appearance of same-sex couples merely participating in marriage, but in reality that is impossible. To accommodate same-sex couples, what is required is redefining marriage in the law to make it conform to the first definition offered above: i.e., making marriage merely the public recognition of a committed relationship for the fulfillment and happiness of adults. That is what has happened in every court decision and every legislative act where marriage has been redefined. What is also not readily apparent is the most serious consequence of redefining marriage: *removing marriage between*

---

4   Congregation for the Doctrine of the Faith (hereafter CDF), Instruction on Respect for Human Life and the Dignity of Procreation *Donum Vitae* (February 22, 1987), A1.

a man and a woman from the law eliminates the only societal institution that unites children with their mothers and fathers.

Redefining marriage to accommodate same-sex couples eliminates all authority for promoting the unique value of men and women marrying before having children. It therefore conflicts with protecting the fundamental internationally recognized human right of children to know and, as far as possible, to be cared for by their mothers and fathers. Anyone promoting that unique value or right would elicit claims of discrimination from people unable to procreate since it would violate the principle of "marriage equality"—equality of relationships.

Well-noted Yale law professor William Eskridge says that redefining marriage "involves the reconfiguration of the family, deemphasizing blood, gender, and kinship ties."[5] Others make the same point by saying it is immoral for the government to promote one kind of parental relationship over another. Notice, this moves the focus away from the right of the child to have a relationship with his or her mother, father and extended family, and puts it on the adults' rights to have a child no matter what. But in reality, who has a right to another person?

Redefining marriage and the family implies the only thing that is important in parenting is competency leading to the notion that no one, including mothers and fathers, are irreplaceable, and men and women are interchangeable. The fallacy of this can be seen by turning to our own experience. All

---

5   William N. Eskridge, Jr., *Gaylaw: Challenging Apartheid In The Closet* (Harvard University Press: Cambridge, MA, 1999).

of us have the desire for connection, for knowing and for being loved by our mother and father.

With marriage redefined, schools would be required to teach marriage as nothing more than an adult-centric institution solely for individual fulfillment. It must be presented as a lifestyle alternative with no relationship to children or the foundation of a family with common ancestors. This will have a profound negative effect on how young people understand marriage, how they approach relationships, and make decisions about marriage and family in their own lives.

The debate about marriage must therefore be shifted to the public interests of each definition: *should marriage continue to be recognized as a human reality that unites a man and a woman with each other and any children born from their union, or should it be redefined as merely the public recognition of a committed relationship for the fulfillment of adults*? What is the public interest of each, and what are the consequences of changing the definition of marriage in the law, particularly on the ability for societal institutions to promote the unique value of encouraging men and women to marry before having children?

While same-sex couples may have sincere and loving relationships, and desire to call them marriages, after careful reflection it becomes obvious that the issue related to the definition of marriage must boil down to the public interest for each of the two conflicting definitions of marriage, and the consequences for redefining marriage in the law. In such a debate, homosexuality or discrimination are no longer factors, nor should they be.

Redefining marriage as merely the public recognition of a committed relationship for the fulfillment of adults, and eliminating the only institution that unites children with their moms and dads must be justified on its merits. What is the public interest of each definition of marriage and the consequences of changing the law to reflect one over the other?

How to deflect common arguments for redefining marriage and maintaining the focus on the reality of marriage is demonstrated in the "Frequently Asked Questions about Redefining Marriage and Related Issues" in Part 6. But first, let's look at the shocking condition of marriage in the U.S. to help us understand that defending marriage is not enough. It is essential to develop a better understanding of what is happening to marriage and to mobilize to rebuild a marriage culture.

❧❧❧

PART 3
Reversing the Breakdown of Marriage that is Touching Almost Every Family

Today, the breakdown of marriage is pervasive. Almost every extended family has children living in families without married mothers and fathers. This is not just caused by divorce, but by the decrease of people actually getting married. In just 30 years the marriage rate per 1000 unmarried women has declined more than 43 percent.[1] Births to unmarried mothers are now over 41 percent among all women and 73 percent among African Americans.[2]

This trend is causing a major problem for society with high human costs. An increased number of children are suffering the consequences of living in poverty and in fatherless homes. Research shows that these conditions put children at risk for negative life-long consequences.

There are many causes for children being raised by single or unmarried parents, but it is not our intention to discuss the causes here. There is one thing, however, that most can agree on.

---

1   Bradford Wilcox, *State of Our Unions, Marriage in America 2011,* The National Marriage Project, University of Virginia, http://www.stateofourunions.org/2011/social_indicators.php.
2   Ibid.

The current situation is intolerable, and a concerted effort for both public and private institutions to work together to promote men and women marrying before having children is needed. Any such effort to reverse the breakdown of marriage and its consequences for children would be forbidden if marriage were redefined, as discussed in Part 2. There would no longer be any institution that specifically unites children with their mothers and fathers to promote. If the institution did not exist, it would have to be created.

A Concern for Every Parent

As already discussed, the premise of "marriage equality" is that all relationships are equal. If marriage is redefined, schools would have to teach marriage as merely a committed relationship for adults with no specific relationship to children and families. Alternative families, such as families without married mothers and fathers, are already being taught in many schools as role models deserving respect. Research shows that 46 percent of eighteen- to twenty-nine-year-olds now believe that the "growing variety in types of family arrangements" is a good thing.[3] This is shocking when you consider that the one thing common to every alternative family is children being deprived of their mother, father, or both. How can this be a good thing? Other research confirms that children are increasingly separating family and children from their understanding of

---

3   Pew Research Center Survey: *The Decline of Marriage and Rise of New Families*, November 18, 2010, http://www.pewsocialtrends.org/2010/11/18/the-decline-of-marriage-and-rise-of-new-families/.

marriage: 56 percent of high school seniors believe it is OK to have children and not be married.[4] An increasing number of eighteen- to twenty-nine-year-olds think that marriage is obsolete (44 percent).[5]

How do these attitudes affect young people's decisions about marriage and family when they reach adulthood? This should be the concern of every parent. Research shows that the percentage of high schools seniors who expressed a desire to marry has remained steady over the years (80 percent girls, 70 percent boys). But something happens between the dreams of teenagers and the altar.

"One of the great social tragedies"

In an article entitled "When Marriage Disappears, the Retreat from Marriage in Middle America," Bradford Wilcox and Elizabeth Marquardt discuss how marriage is collapsing among the lower and middle class. The reasons are varied and complex but one thing they cite is how marriage is now viewed as what they describe as the "soul mate" model. It has become a couple-centered vehicle for personal growth, emotional intimacy, and shared consumption that depends for its survival on the happiness of both spouses. It is viewed as a luxury when couples can afford it and non-essential to children and family.[6]

---

4   Bradford Wilcox, *State of our Unions, Marriage in America 2009,* data from University of Michigan, http://www.stateofourunions.org/2009/index.php.

5   Pew: *The Decline of Marriage and Rise of New Families.*

6   Bradford Wilcox, "When Marriage Disappears" *State of Our Unions, 2010,* The National Marriage Project, University of Virginia, http://stateofourunions.org/2010/SOOU 2010.php.

This is another way of expressing what was described in Part 2, the understanding of marriage as merely the public recognition of a committed relationship for the fulfillment of the spouses.

By contrast, Wilcox and Marquardt indicate less and less young people are "identifying with an 'institutional' model of marriage, which seeks to integrate sex, parenthood, economic cooperation, and emotional intimacy in a permanent union."[7] This is the sociologist description of marriage, the human reality that unites a man and a woman with each other and any children born from their union.

An Imperative of Social Justice

The significant decline in marriage and increase in non-marital pregnancies is largely occurring among the poor and less educated, creating a new class divide. "It is one of the great social tragedies of our time that marriage is flourishing among the most advantaged and self-actualized groups in our society and waning among those who could most benefit from its economic and child-rearing partnership."[8]

Note the quick facts in the Appendix about the breakdown of marriage and its human consequences. Considering these and other consequences of the breakdown of marriage, it becomes an imperative of social justice for children to support public policies and cultural influences that include the following:

7   Ibid.
8   Ibid.

1. Promoting men and women marrying before having children
2. Changing curricula and other cultural influences that undermine young people's understanding of the true meaning of love, friendship, human sexuality, family, and marriage
3. Researching and addressing the other impediments to marriage

For starters, it is important to help people understand the seriousness of the breakdown of marriage and its consequences, and the importance of having policies and public support to reverse this trend. This can never happen if marriage is redefined to eliminate the only institution that unites children with their moms and dads.

It is critical to unite to build a movement to evaluate every public and private societal institution on the basis of how well it supports and promotes marriage and the family. This is common sense, and it is also the teaching of the Catholic Church.[9] Accepting this teaching does not require faith. It is a reasonable solution to a tragic societal problem that affects the development and lives of millions of people.

---

9   Pontifical Council for Justice and Peace, Compendium of the Social Doctrine of the Catholic Church (2004), nos. 252-254.

ॐ

PART 4
Questions to Pose and Ponder about the Rights of Children

Most are quite familiar with arguments supporting the redefinition of marriage. Many have been confronted with the tough questions that create confusion about the reality of marriage and its purpose, and are used to justify accommodating the aspirations of the "gay rights" movement. These questions and how to respond to them will be addressed in Part 6, "Frequently Asked Questions." However, there are other questions about marriage and its relationship to the fundamental human rights of children that also must be asked in a respectful way.

Although they may seem counter-cultural at first, these questions are important to provoke thought, and to open new kinds of discussions about the reality of marriage and family. They help reveal the dignity and rights of the child and stimulate contemplation in search for the truth about the human person, marriage and family.

Some of these questions may provoke very deep feelings that may be difficult for some to deal with, and may require time for reflection. They are not meant to put someone on the spot or to be used in ways that could imply criticism or judgment about something that someone has done in the past. As a society, we have all fallen short of God's plan for marriage and human sexuality. It is time to recognize our collective brokenness and to begin working together to build a more just and humane society. The past is past. The focus now must be on rebuilding a marriage culture and protecting, as far as possible, the rights of children and the best interests of society for the future.

Consider these questions:

1. **Does a child have a fundamental human right to know and, as far as possible, be cared for by his or her mother and father?**

   - Consider, everyone without exception has a mother and father. Does that fact have a significance that goes beyond biology?

   - Consider the common desire we all have to know, and to be cared for and loved by the man and woman from whom we originated. Those relationships are part of our identity—not just with our mom and dad, but brothers and sisters, grandparents, aunts, uncles and cousins.

   - Consider: Men and women have a fundamental human right to procreate.[1] However, it is common sense (and Catholic teaching) that because of the potential for conflict between the child's right to be born into a real

---

1   The human right to procreate is also recognized in the *Skinner v. Oklahoma Supreme Court decision,* 316 U.S. 535, 536 (62 S.Ct. 1110, 86 L.Ed. 1655). See also, Blessed Pope John Paul II, Encyclical Letter on the Hundredth Anniversary of Rerum Novarum *Centesimus Annus* (May 1, 1991), 154B.

family united with his or her mother and father, men and women have a responsibility to only intentionally procreate after they have made themselves irreplaceable to each other through marriage.[2]

2. **Do you think it would be good to have a public institution that specifically unites children with their moms and dads or promotes they be raised by their moms and dads together?**

    - **If YES,** that institution already exists—it is called marriage. If it did not exist as a natural institution that can be recognized by all, it would have to be invented *(not as a matter of usefulness or societal benefit, but as a matter of charity and justice for children).*[3]

    - **If NO,** the question becomes, "How can anyone justify opposing the only institution that unites kids with their moms and dads?" (Note: People may have a tendency to shift the discussion to families with same-sex parents. This moves it away from marriage to the topic of parenting children who have lost or been separated from their moms or dads or both. Marriage is not a requirement for adoption or parenting a child. This is discussed further in Part 5, "Avoiding Common Traps").

2   CDF, *Donum Vitae*, A1; Blessed Pope John XXIII, Encyclical Letter on Establishing Universal Peace in Truth, Justice, Charity, and Liberty *Pacem in Terris* (April 11, 1963) nos. 16, 17, 28, 30, "rights and duties".

3   *Donum Vitae,* A1.

- Consider: In 2009, the U.S. Justice Department stated in a brief that "The government does not contend that there are legitimate government interests in 'creating a legal structure that promotes the raising of children by both of their biological parents . . ."[4] **Do you think this is true?**

3. **Does anyone have a right to create a child with the intention of depriving him or her of knowing and being cared for by the child's mother or father or both?**
   - Consider the reality of persons conceived by sperm or egg donors, or through the use of surrogates to produce a child for someone else. The reality is that these people search for their anonymous fathers and mothers and brothers and sisters—they are part of that person's identity.
   - Consider: Does anyone have a right to a child? Does anyone have a right to another person?

4. **Should government, schools and other societal institutions promote the unique value of men and women marrying before having children?**
   - Consider the human consequences of the breakdown of marriage on poverty, delinquency, dropout rates, gang membership, incarceration rates, etc. *It is a sociological*

---

4   *Smelts v. United States* (Doc. 42 at 8-9).

tragedy with real human costs. Lives are compromised and many are not able to achieve their potential. Do we have an obligation to future generations? Do we need to work towards rebuilding a marriage culture to reverse this trend?

- Consider: Scholars from the liberal Brookings Institution[5] and the conservative Heritage Foundation[6] have suggested programs geared to change behavior to promote marriage. Examples of other such behavior-changing efforts include: anti-smoking, say no to drugs, wear seatbelts, respect the environment, eat healthy foods, get exercise, etc. Do you think changing public behavior and attitudes about the importance of marriage that unites kids with their moms and dads is as important as anti-obesity and anti-smoking campaigns?

- Consider: While some public policy scholars encourage programs and institutions that promote marriage that unites children with their moms and dads,[7] others say it discriminates against gays because it promotes one type of family (in which children are united with their parents) over another (in which children are deprived of their mother or father or both). What do you think? Is it discriminatory to have a policy that uniquely encourages men and woman to marry before having children?

---

5   Ron Haskins and Isabel Sawhill, *Creating an Opportunity Society* (Brookings Institution, 2009).

6   Rector, "Marriage," Heritage Foundation.

7   Haskins, *Opportunity Society*.

∞⊙⊙∞

PART 5

Avoiding Common Traps That Hinder Communications for Advocating Public Policy about Marriage and Family

1. Use two conflicting understandings of marriage.

Always focus the discussion on the public interest regarding these two conflicting definitions of marriage:

    a. Is marriage merely an institution for public recognition of committed relationships (for adult fulfillment), or

    b. Is marriage an institution that unites a man and a woman with each other and any children born from their union?

These two definitions are very different and are incompatible with each other. The first definition is what effectively must be incorporated in the law to permit marriage by same-sex couples.

The problem is that most people today understand marriage as merely the public recognition of a committed relationship between a man and a woman that creates an ideal situation for rearing children. This understanding makes it difficult to defend marriage between a man and a woman except on the basis of tradition, biblical truth, complementarity, or outcomes in parenting.

But that first definition is not what marriage is. It is much more. It is a human reality, that when recognized by individual men and women by their free choices, *marriage unites them with each other and any children born from their unions.* That is what it is; that is what it does. It is a fact.

The explanation of this phrase in Part 2 bears repeating: It "describes the communion of man and woman leading to a communion between parent and child." It "describes an intimate community of life and love, and expresses procreation, complementarity, motherhood and fatherhood, irreplaceability, non-substitutability, kinship, family, the good of children, *and even the potential for the heartbreak of infertility"*—the totality of what marriage is.

More importantly, describing marriage in this way presents it as something that correlates with common human experience of each and therefore of all—the experience of longing for connection with and for knowing our mother and father.

Because of the influences of the culture that have changed how the majority understands love, human sexuality, marriage and family, it is difficult for many to understand what marriage is, its public interest, and the consequences of redefining it without contrasting the two conflicting definitions and seeking an understanding of the public interest of each.

In addition to clarifying the issue, notice that homosexuality ceases to be a factor. If a case can be made to redefine marriage as merely the public recognition of a committed relationship for the benefit of adults, there could be little justification for depriving same-sex couples of participation. However, there is a compelling case for continuing to recognize reality of marriage between a man and a woman that unites them with each other and any children born from their union.

2. The term "same-sex marriage" is a trap.

Never use the term "gay marriage" or "same-sex marriage." Use of the term "gay marriage" or "same-sex marriage" implies participation in marriage by same-sex couples. It obscures the fact that in order to accommodate same-sex couples, marriage must actually be redefined in the law as merely the public recognition of a committed relationship and marriage between a man and a woman, the only institution that unites children with their mothers and fathers must be eliminated.

Therefore it would be more accurate to describe the issue as "redefining marriage to accommodate same-sex couples."

Removing the only institution that unites children with their mothers and fathers presumes there is no public interest in any such institution, which is untrue, particularly when one considers the consequences of the breakdown of marriage. Additionally and surprisingly to many, redefining marriage would make it legally discriminatory for public and private institutions to promote the unique value of children being united with their moms and dads, since it would violate the principle of equality of relationships and equality in parenting.

3. Avoid arguing what is "good" for children.

This may be surprising, but don't talk about what is "good" for children or what they "need."

Avoid saying things like, "Children need a mother and father"; "A child needs mother love and father love"; or "Having a married mother and father is good for children."

These examples may express something that is true, but they present two problems. First, what is "good" or what is "needed" is subjective—depending on the perspective of the other person. Some think all that children need is a loving couple, or just someone who loves them. Indeed, children raised by single parents and even same-sex couples adapt and have good outcomes as reflected in some social science studies. Some people will respond that many children even do better with same-sex couples than those raised by their own married mothers and fathers. Since the "good" of the child is subjective and debatable, the discussion gravitates away from the reality of marriage uniting children with their moms and dads to competency in parenting. Competency in parenting, of course, has nothing to do with the definition of marriage.

The second problem is more subtle. Notice when people speak about children needing *a* mother and *a* father, one may assume they are referring to the child's mother and father, but some hear that as a social role of mother and father rather than specific persons. It is children's actual mother and father who are irreplaceable and are part of their identity. This may seem trivial, but consider that a key argument for redefining marriage and family is that gender roles are interchangeable when it comes to child rearing.

Instead, focus on the fact that every child has a mother and father, and that they have a fundamental human right to know and, as far as possible, to be cared for by *their* mother and father. It is therefore reasonable that a child has a right to be born into a family with a mother and father who have first made themselves irreplaceable to each other through marriage.[1] This right can be verified as true by turning to the common *desire* everyone has for relationship with the man and woman from whom they originated. It is part of one's identity.

4. Don't let the discussion shift from marriage to competency of parenting.

As discussed in #3 above, it is easy for conversations about marriage to shift to a discussion about competency in parenting. Remember, every child has a mother and a father. Children who have lost or have been separated from their mothers or fathers or both are parented or adopted by others as a matter of charity. Marriage is not a requirement for parenting. However, marriage between a man and a woman is the only institution that unites kids with their moms and dads. That is the only public interest for the civil recognition of marriage and for public and private institutions to promote it.

5. Avoid using biology or social science to justify marriage between a man and a woman.

The truth about the human person, marriage and family can never be known through the sciences.

Biology can tell us that a man and a woman are biologically incomplete without each other and in the conjugal act they

---

1   *Donum Vitae*, A1.

become a single human organism. The philosopher/moral theologian Germain Grisez beautifully expresses this reality: "The bodies which become one flesh in sexual intercourse are persons; their unity in a certain sense forms a single person, the *potential* procreator from whom a new human individual flows."[2] But this is not what makes marriage. Marriage is the recognition of this reality by the state, culture, religions and the individual man and woman. By their free choice, they make themselves irreplaceable to each other in marriage and commit themselves to the common good of the union in preparation to receive new life as a gift of equal value and dignity to themselves.[3]

Social science studies may show that "children do best with a mother and father," but this evidence should not be used as an argument for defining marriage in the law. It should only be used in combination with demographic data for elucidating people on the consequences of the breakdown of marriage and the imperative of laws and public institutions promoting the marriage of men and women before they have children. If social science studies are used to defend marriage, the discussion will inevitably lead to competency in parenting, not marriage.

Social science cannot tell us about the intrinsic dignity of the person, the desires of the heart, what love is, or the primordial relationship between mother and father and child.

---

2 *Germain Grisez,* quoted by William E. May, *Marriage: the Rock on Which the Family is Built* (Ignatius Press: San Francisco, 2009), 73.

3 William E. May, *Marriage: the Rock on Which the Family is Built* (Ignatius Press: San Francisco, 2009), chap. 1.

6. Don't say "we believe," when you mean "we know."

"Believe" is a word with many meanings. How we use it can lead to misunderstandings in this age of relativism—"what is true for you is not true for me." Saying "we believe" can be interpreted as "we aren't sure" or "it is only true for people who hold a particular belief." "Believing" **is** "knowing" something from a trusted source. Never use "believe" when you can use "know." It forces us to think about what we really know and how we know it, and what we aren't sure of.

For example, when we say, "As Catholics, we believe marriage can only be between a man and a woman," how is that interpreted by our children and friends? "This is true for Catholics, but it may not be true for anyone else?" Or, "This is an article of faith that we Catholics are trying to impose on society?"

However, this is not an article of faith based on revelation. We *know* marriage unites a man and a woman with each other and any children born from their union. It is a fact. We know this is a reality that cannot be created or changed, only recognized. Knowing this is not dependent on belief in God. We *know* marriage is the only institution that unites kids with their moms and dads. That is a fact.

7. Avoid debates about homosexuality.

Avoid the temptation to debate sexual ethics and the morality of homosexuality in relation to public policy about marriage and family. This is not to say that sexual ethics is not an important topic for rebuilding a marriage culture, but as demonstrated in the arguments expressed in the preceding parts of this guide, the issue of homosexuality and sexual ethics has (or should have), surprisingly, very little relevance to the public policy debate about marriage. This will be demonstrated further in Part 6, the Frequently Asked Questions.

Introducing discussions about homosexuality, gay lifestyles, sexual ethics and personal behavior can lead to misunderstanding and distractions. Proponents of redefining marriage try to draw marriage advocates into such discussions because they shift the debate away from marriage to the fair treatment of homosexuals. **The reality of marriage and the consequences of redefining it must be the sole focus of the public policy discussion.**

Promotion of any improper response to the sexual urge harms everyone, whether they are attracted to the same-sex or not. It leads people to reduce others to objects of use, violating their dignity, and undermining their quest for love, intimacy and friendship. This is a problem that contributes to the breakdown of marriage among men and women, and must be dealt with as part of the overall effort to rebuild a marriage culture.

8. Don't use religiously based arguments.

It is not appropriate to use religious doctrine or quotes from Scripture to justify public policy positions about marriage and family.

Not only would it make an ineffective argument, but imposing an article of faith on persons or society would conflict with the freedom for religious expression of others. That would be unconstitutional and would be contrary to Catholic teaching.

Public policy arguments must always be based on reason purified by faith.[4] *Marriage is a human reality—an institution based on recognizing the characteristic that distinguishes it from every other relationship—the foundation of the natural family.* That is why it has been recognized in different ways by every culture, society and religion.

Catholic teachings and Scripture do not create reality but provide a deeper understanding of what is real for believers, those who trust Christ and His Church.

9. Don't use ideological terms.

Unfortunately, many see public policy issues about marriage and family through ideological lenses and view positions as either liberal or conservative. They are neither, but based in reality that all can recognized as true regardless of one's political point of view. As the renowned biographer of Pope John Paul II, George Weigel has written, "the Catholic Church is about true-and-false, not liberal-and-conservative."[5] Avoid using ideological labels when discussing public policy on marriage.

---

4   Pope Benedict XVI, Encyclical Letter on Christian Love *Deus Caritas Est* (December 25, 2005), no. 28.
5   George Weigel, "Catholics and Modernity," *National Review Online,* July 12, 2012, http://www.nationalreview.com/articles/309256/catholics-and-modernity-george-weigel.

PART 6

Frequently Asked Questions about Redefining Marriage and Related Issues

6.1. GETTING OFF ON THE RIGHT FOOT

Q-1 *Why do you oppose "same-sex marriage"?*

A   I don't oppose "same-sex marriage"; I oppose redefining marriage to accommodate same-sex couples. There is a big difference. While I am sympathetic to the sincere and loving same-sex couples who desire to marry, the consequences of redefining marriage are too great.

Q-2 *What is the difference between opposing "same-sex marriage" and opposing redefining marriage?*

A   Marriage between a man and a woman is an institution that not only unites them with each other but with any children born from their union. To accommodate the demands of the "gay rights" movement, marriage would have to be redefined as merely the legal recognition of a committed relationship for the fulfillment of adults. Removing marriage between a man and a woman from the law eliminates the only institution that unites children with their moms and dads.

Q-3 *Same-sex couples don't want to redefine marriage; they just want to participate in it.*

A Same-sex couples cannot participate in marriage unless it is redefined as merely the public recognition of a committed relationship. But that is not what marriage is. It is much more. Marriage unites a man and a woman with each other and any children born from their union. That's a fact that can only be recognized and never changed.

Q-4 *Why can't the two definitions of marriage co-exist so that everyone can just be happy?*

A With the decline of marriage, and more and more children being deprived of their basic right to know and be raised by their mom and dad, it is critical for public and private institutions to promote the unique value of men and women marrying before having children. The concept of "marriage equality" is that committed relationships between same-sex and opposite sex couples must be publicly recognized as equal in value to society. This would make it discriminatory for public and private institutions to promote the unique public interest of marriage between a man and a woman. Marriage would have to be taught in schools as being separate and distinct from children and family, or just one lifestyle alternative if someone wants to have a child.

Q-5 *I have a child who is gay. Everyone wants their children in stable committed and loving relationships. Don't they have a right to be happy too?*

A   What is it that you seek or your child seeks for him or herself? Is it not true love and true friendship? True love is not a matter of a legal contract, but a matter of the will—a commitment to be directed toward the flourishing of the other and to receive the other as a gift of infinite value and dignity. This is what leads to happiness, not a legal contract or the word "marriage." True love is not always easy and requires virtue to really understand what contributes to the flourishing of the other. In fact, true love can often lead to suffering. When one makes happiness the objective of a relationship, the other person is reduced to an object whose purpose is to produce happiness. When one person ceases to be happy, the basis for the relationship is no more—i.e., there never was love and commitment to start with.[1]

Q-6 *Gays want to marry for the same reason heterosexual couples want to marry. Don't gays have the right to love the people they choose?*

A   Everyone is made for love, but not everyone is made for marriage. While love, being directed toward the good of the other, is important in marriage, there is

---

1   Karol Wojtyla (Blessed Pope John Paul II) *Love and Responsibility*, (Ignatius Press: San Francisco 1993) chap. 1.

no public interest in defining the only institution that unites children with their moms and dads out of existence merely to create in its place an institution solely for memorializing a loving relationship for the benefit of adults. ***NOTE ABOUT CIVIL UNIONS: Don't be tempted to suggest that pseudo-marriage (civil unions or domestic partnerships) are an acceptable alternative for same-sex couples. They create confusion about the reality of marriage and reinforce that marriage is nothing more than the public recognition of a committed relationship for adults. (See Section 12.*** **CIVIL UNIONS AND DOMESTIC PARTNERSHIPS.*)**

Q-7   *Not letting same-sex couples marry violates their civil rights. It is unfair and discriminatory.*

A   There are two conflicting understandings of what marriage is. Some believe it is merely the public recognition of a committed relationship between adults. If that is all marriage is, we can agree it would be discriminatory to prevent same-sex couples from marrying because there would be no rational basis to restrict it to a man and a woman. It would not be connected to having children and family. Marriage, however, is much more. Marriage unites a man and a woman with each other and any children born from their union. It is a reality that can only be recognized by law and not changed.

Note: Gay rights groups are no longer arguing that same-sex couples should have the right to marry to have the benefit of hospital visiting privileges should a partner become ill. Federal regulations that took effect in 2011 require hospitals to permit patients to designate selected individuals to have the same rights and privileges as family members. This regulation benefits all single people with close friends, including priests and members of religious orders.

6.2.   TIME FOR CAPITULATION AND ENDING THE CULTURE WAR?

Q-8   *"Same-sex marriage" is inevitable. It is already legal in a number of states and public opinion polls indicate that more and more people support it.*

A   Every time "traditional" marriage has been on the ballot, the voters have supported it. Those trying to redefine marriage have never had an electoral victory—not one win. In fact, in many of the states that have redefined marriage, voters have been denied the right to vote on marriage. In court cases in which traditional marriage was overturned, the courts have considered marriage as merely the public recognition of a committed relationship for adult fulfillment.

As a matter of justice and protection of the human rights of children, it is essential that marriage, the only public institution that unites children with their mothers and fathers, be restored in every jurisdiction where it has been eliminated.

Q-9   *We are living in a society where everyone needs to get along and just accept each other. It is time to stop denigrating and stigmatizing same-sex relationships. In the interest of peace, let's just end the culture war and let same-sex couples marry.*

A   This assumes that the marriage debate is merely about the interests of adults, and ignores the interest and rights of children to be born into a real family with a married mother and father. Too many children are deprived of that right today. It is essential for laws to not only recognize the only institution that unites children with their mothers and fathers, but actively promote the unique value of men and woman marrying before having children.

Unfortunately, there has been too much vitriol in the debate related to marriage on both sides. There has been too much focus on homosexuality and the interest of adults which have little to do with public interest of the only institution that unites children with their mothers and fathers.

Q-10 *Instead of fighting over marriage, people on both sides of the debate should settle their differences and work to strengthen marriage.*

A   It is critical to change laws and adopt policies that reduce the decline of marriage, which contributes to more children living in poverty and the tragic consequences of children from fatherless homes. Reversing this trend requires the education of young people on the reality of marriage that unites a man and a woman with each other and any children born from their union. It also requires teaching that it is wrong to intentionally have a child outside of marriage. Alternative families in which children are deprived of married mothers and fathers must be discouraged. Schools must teach the proper response to the sexual urge, the true meaning of love, and how to develop the kind of relationships that lead to healthy marriages. All of these are in conflict with the proposals to redefine marriage, promote families without married mothers and fathers, and advocate curricula and policies that separate sex from procreation and marriage.

6.3. ALTERNATIVE FAMILIES, GAY PARENTING, AND PROCREATION

Q-11 *Why should marriage privilege one type of family over another? Isn't that discriminatory?*

A   Every child has a fundamental human right to know and, as far as possible, to be cared for by his or her mom and dad. Marriage is the only institution that promotes that interest. It is also in the public interest (recognized by the *U.N. Convention on the Rights of the Child*, Art. 7, 9).

Q-12 *Same-sex couples have families too. Don't their children have a right to married parents?*

A   This changes the subject from marriage to parenting a child who has been separated from their mother, father or both. It is always a tragedy when this happens because mothers and fathers are part of the child's identity and contribute to their development. However, when this does happen, as a matter of charity, other people step in to parent them. They do not have to be married. It could be a single family member or others.

Q-13 *Same-sex couples can have their own children. Why should they be deprived of marriage?*

A   This question is not related to marriage either, but it raises another ethical concern. Every person without exception has a mother and father. When a child is created with a sperm or egg donor, this amounts to the intentional privation for the child of knowing and being cared for by his or her mother or father or both, a violation of a fundamental human right of the child.

Q-14 *Are you saying that families with unmarried parents or gay parents are illegitimate or are inferior to families with a married mother and father?*

A   Not at all. One must presume everyone who is parenting tries to do the very best job they can. Some may do an even better job than some married parents, but in reality, children in those situations have lost something common to every child that is related to their identity and development—hardly an ideal situation. It is important to recognize that anyone who is parenting has a very difficult and important job.

Q-15 *Same-sex couples and single people have just as much a right to have a child as anyone else.*

A   No one has a right to another person. Does anyone have a right to you? Thinking that way treats a child as property instead of a gift—a person of equal value and dignity to the adult. Everyone has a fundamental right to procreate, but unless that is done within a marriage bond, it conflicts with the fundamental right of the child to be born into a family, and to know and be cared for by both his and her mother and father. It is wrong to intentionally deprive a child of that right without just cause. This is common sense and can be confirmed by our own desire for connection with the man and woman from whom we originated.[2]

Q-16 *Some same-sex couples do a better job at parenting than many mothers and fathers.*

A It is faulty reasoning to compare the best of one vs. the worst of another.

Note: Proponents of redefining marriage often try to support their position by focusing on competence of parents and outcomes of children. This moves the discussion away from marriage to parenting children who have lost or been separated from their moms, dads or both. Many fail to notice the shift and try to argue outcomes based on social science. Marriage is not about who can parent best. The sole public interest for recognizing the reality of marriage is that it unites children with their moms and dads. This corresponds with the interest and the human right of the child.

Q-17 *Isn't the situation with an infertile couple in marriage the same as a same-sex couple? They can't have children.*

A Not all married men and women have children, but every child has a mom and a dad, and marriage is the

---

2   CDF, *Donum Vitae,* A1 and *Legal Recognition of Homosexual Unions,* 7; Blessed John Paul II, *Centesimus Annus,*154b; Blessed John XXIII, *Pacem in Terris* nos. 16, 17, 28.

only institution that unites them in a family. That is the primary public interest for marriage.

Q-18 *When you say the only public interest in marriage is that it is the only institution that unites children with their moms and dads, doesn't that ignore many other benefits of marriage?*

A   Yes, there are many benefits and goods of marriage, but the fact that it unites a man and a woman with each other and any children born from their union is the sole reason that marriage has been recognized as a reality by every culture, every society, and every religion—each in their own way. United families are the first and fundamental cell of society—the first school of love, peace and justice. Marriage, their foundation, must be supported by laws and school curricula. In fact, every institution in society must be evaluated by how well it supports marriage and the family.[3]

6.4.   WHAT DIFFERENCE WOULD IT MAKE TO YOUR MARRIAGE

Q-19 *How will letting same-sex couples marry affect your marriage?*

A   It won't, but it will have an impact on how marriage will be taught in schools and how children understand its

---

3   CCC, pt. 3 chap. 2 art.1; Blessed John Paul II, *Letter to Families,* nos. 7, 17; Blessed John XXXIII, *Pacem in Terris,* no. 16.

meaning and purpose as the foundation of the family. Changing the law to accommodate same-sex couples requires marriage to be taught in schools as merely the public recognition of a committed relationship with no connection to children and family. (See Part 2, *What is "same-sex marriage."*) This will affect the attitudes young people will have about marriage and family and will likely affect decisions they make about marriage, children and family in their lives.

Note: Creating pseudo marriages like civil unions and domestic partnerships would have the same effect. (See Frequently Asked Questions in Section 12, CIVIL UNIONS AND DOMESTIC PARTNERSHIPS.)

Q-20 *Heterosexuals have already made a mess of marriage with high divorce rates and out of wedlock births. How would letting same-sex couples marry make that any worse?*

A   Marriage is in crisis with severe societal consequences including the increase in fatherless homes and children living in poverty. Reforms to encourage men and women to marry before having children and supporting them in staying married are badly needed. Redefining marriage in a way that disconnects it from children and family would not only prohibit promoting the unique value of uniting children with their mothers and fathers, but would make it discriminatory for public and private institutions to do so. This would open the door to lawsuits and the threat of government penalties for promoting marriage. (See Part 2, *What is "same-sex marriage"?*)

6.5.   CIVIL MARRIAGE vs. RELIGIOUS MARRIAGE

Q-21   Why not create two distinct kinds of marriages in the law, civil marriage regulated by the state and religious marriage regulated by religions?

A   The state and religions recognize the same reality that marriage unites a man and a woman with each other and any children born from their union. They just recognize it in different ways according to their competencies. The state regulates the public interest aspects: age of consent, distance in blood relationship, no other existing marriages, etc. Religions may have different qualifications based on the precepts of a particular faith.[4]

Q-22   Why not get the state out of the marriage business and just have religious (or private) marriage? It would increase the value of religious marriage.

A   Civil law recognizes marriage as a human reality which is connected to a fundamental human right of children and the public interest in promoting that men and women marry before having children. Without marriage being defined in the law as a union of a man and a woman,

---

4   CCC 1603.

public institutions would have no authority, and thus would be prevented from promoting the public interest of marriage and the rights of children connected to it, because it would be deemed to be discriminatory against same-sex couples. Marriage not only protects the welfare of children but also that of mothers. The human and social costs of marriage breakdown have a direct relationship to the number of children living in poverty and to abuse and neglect of children. Laws and public institutions should be judged by how well they support marriage and the family.

6.6. CHURCH AND STATE, FUNDAMENTAL RIGHT TO MARRY, AND INTERRACIAL MARRIAGE

Q-23 *Why is the Catholic Church trying to impose its beliefs about marriage on society?*

A   Catholics must never try to impose an article of faith on others. That would be a violation of dignity of the person and the right to religious freedom. However, the Church is right to provide moral guidance in the defense of the dignity of the person, marriage as the foundation of the family, and the fundamental human right of children to be born into a family with a married mother and father.[5] The organization of secular society is not the work of the Church, but of politics. Participation in

---

5   *Donum Vitae*, A1.

this work is the role of laity using reasoning purified by faith. This reasoning can be known to all independent of faith or belief in God.[6]

See Q-21 response re state and religion recognizing the same reality.

Q-24 *Marriage has been evolving over time. It was redefined when polygamy and bans on interracial marriage were removed. Permitting same-sex couples to marry is just one more step in an ever changing institution. It is progress.*

A   The changes in marriage were not redefinitions of marriage. Both recognize that marriage unites a man and a woman with each other and any children born from their union. Polygamy is merely one man and marriages to multiple women, Every child has a married mother and father in a polygamous marriage. But polygamy is unjust and harmful to women and children.

According to Catholic teaching, polygamy is "contrary to the equal personal dignity of men and women who in matrimony give themselves with a love that is total and therefore unique and exclusive."[7]

---

6   *Deus Caritas Est,* no. 28.
7   CCC 2387.

Q-25 *Discrimination against gays and lesbians is similar to the discrimination against blacks when interracial marriage was once banned in the U.S.*

A   There is no connection. History reveals that the reason for bans on interracial marriage was entirely based in eugenics—maintaining racial purity. It is inconceivable today that the belief by many in the early to mid 20th century was that permitting interracial marriage would cause the end of the white race since "one drop of black blood" would make a person black. Up until the 1960s it was very unusual for people to procreate outside of wedlock, so banning interracial marriage had the effect of banning procreation (*Loving v. Virginia*—U.S. Supreme Court).

Q-26 *There is a fundamental right to marry. Banning marriage for same-sex couples violates that right.*

A   When the U.S. Supreme Court struck down bans on interracial marriage, they did find that there was a fundamental right to marry, but a close reading of the decision makes it clear that the right was tied to the fundamental right to procreate, since at that time, it was unusual for someone to procreate outside of marriage. A ban on marriage was essentially a ban on the right to procreate, which provided the basis for striking down anti-miscegenation laws. Therefore this case does not apply to same-sex couples (*Loving v. Virginia*—U.S. Supreme Court).

6.7.   ADOPTION

Q-27   *Why does the Catholic Church say gay adoptions do violence to children? That is an outrageous example of discrimination.*

A   A careful reading of the document, *Considerations on the Legal Recognition of Homosexual Unions* will reveal that the Church is not talking about physical violence, but a violation of the dignity of children who have already been deprived of their mothers and fathers. Placing them in a home with a same-sex couple is a second privation—this time a privation of the experience of being raised by adoptive mothers and fathers, the only people who can legitimately stand in for the mothers and fathers of whom the children have already been deprived.

Q-28   *But single people can adopt. And, wouldn't it better for a child to have a stable home with loving parents rather than being left in an orphanage or foster care?*

A   Justice for the child would best be served by adoption by a man and a woman who have first made themselves irreplaceable to each other through marriage. This is what prepares them to receive life as a gift, either from their own union or by adoption. Sometimes there are more children in need of adoption than married men and women willing to adopt. Justice would best be served by encouraging more married men and women to adopt.

6.8.   LOVE, SEXUALITY AND DISCRIMINATION

Q-29 *Why does the Catholic Church condemn gays and lesbians?*

A   The Church condemns no one; only God can judge. The Church teaches the inviolable dignity of each and every person as a manifestation of God's love. It is because of this dignity that every person must be treated with respect and dignity, and free from unjust discrimination.

Catechism §2358: "The number of men and women who have deep-seated homosexual tendencies is not negligible. This inclination, which is objectively disordered, constitutes for most of them a trial. They must be accepted with respect, compassion, and sensitivity. Every sign of unjust discrimination in their regard should be avoided."

Q-30 *Doesn't the Catechism teach that homosexuality is a disorder?*

A   This is a source of misunderstanding and pain for many. The Catechism teaches that homosexual acts are intrinsically disordered, not the persons. It is a precise philosophical term that refers to acts that do not coincide with the order of nature for propagating life. It is possible for men and women to engage in the same type of acts as heterosexual couples, and those are intrinsically disordered for the same reason. In either case, it is not only an offense against God, but is harmful to the people involved because it is an act of use of the person and therefore a violation of his or her dignity.

Q-31 *People who oppose "same-sex marriage" claim that love between same-sex couples is inferior to that between men and woman. Gays can love just like anyone else.*

A All human persons are made for love, but not everyone is made for marriage. Many confuse sexual relations with love. While they can provide an illusion of intimacy, persons can easily be reduced to mere objects of use, even in marriage. When a relationship devolves into a contract of mutual use, it is contrary to love, intimacy and friendship. In these cases, the love, intimacy and friendship which are sincerely sought become difficult or impossible to achieve.[8]

"Without love man is incomprehensible to himself."[9]

Q-32 *Heterosexuals get to have the pleasure of sex; is it fair to say homosexuals can't? Why should they be left out?*

A The sexual urge is common to everyone, so the question becomes how to respond to it and to gain mastery over it for the sake of achieving true love and intima-

8 Blessed John Paul II, *Love and Responsibility*, chap. 1.
9 Blessed John Paul II, Encyclical Letter on The Redeemer of Man *Redemptor Hominus* (March 4, 1979), no. 10.

cy. When pleasure becomes the end that is sought, the human person (body and soul) is reduced to a means or an object of use. **Using a person is the opposite of love.** Use degrades the person and violates their intrinsic dignity whether they realize it or not, or whether they consent to it or not. Love and intimacy cannot be achieved between a person and an object, only between two subjects (actors) of equal value and dignity. Considering the harm in reducing another person to an object of use, chastity becomes an act of love rather than being viewed merely as self-deprivation. This may be difficult to accept, but when considered with an open mind, it is common sense.[10]

6.9.   CONFLICT WITH FREEDOM OF CONSCIENCE / RELIGIOUS EXPRESSION

Q-33   *Redefining marriage would not affect religions: the First Amendment of the U.S. Constitution prohibits any law that would interfere with the free exercise of religion. Therefore the state could not force religions, or priests, ministers, rabbis or imams to marry people in conflict with their faiths.*

A   It is true that clergy could not be compelled to marry people who do not qualify under the tenets of their faith. However,   churches, synagogues, mosques, or

---

10   Blessed John Paul II, *Love and Responsibility,* chap. 3.

religious organization like the Knights of Columbus could be sued for discrimination if they fail to rent or provide access to their facilities or non-religious services to same-sex couples that they make available to other individuals or community organizations (sports leagues, charities, private parties, etc.). They could also be threatened with the elimination of tax exemptions as punishment for discrimination. These might include "wedding" receptions, anniversary parties, or other events. Churches try to teach and form young people in the real meaning of marriage. To be forced to recognize such events by providing space or services for them would conflict with the exercise of one's faith and would cause scandal and confusion to the congregation.

Q-34   *Changing marriage to permit same-sex couples to marry won't affect anyone else adversely.*

A   Marriage is a reality that can only be recognized and never changed. If laws are changed to redefine marriage, anyone who adheres to the reality of what marriage is and refuses to acknowledge an unjust and unreasonable law will be defined as discriminatory under the law and subjected to persecution, loss of employment or advancement opportunities, and in some cases legal action. Children who do not accept marriage as it has been redefined will also be subjected to persecution and potential bullying.

6.10. MARRIAGE AND PROCREATION / INFERTILITY

Q-35 *Marriage can't be about procreation because not all men and women in marriage procreate.*

A   Not all men and women in marriage have children, but every child has a mother and father. Marriage is the only institution that unites children with their moms and dads, and for that reason it is a good that must be protected by law and promoted as a matter of public policy.

Q-36 *Why let people who can't procreate or are beyond child bearing age marry?*

A   The public good for recognizing marriage in civil law is to promote uniting children with their moms and dads, and to help protect the welfare of children and their mothers. For a valid marriage, it must be consummated, meaning the man and the woman must engage in a sexual act that is procreative in nature irrespective of fecundity (or fruitfulness of the act). By doing this, they provide a good role model, helping reinforce the norm of engaging in procreative acts only within marriage, thereby strengthening the only institution that unites children with their moms and dads.

Also, men and women who are infertile have many options for living their marital vocation of love, including making a child irreplaceable to them through adoption. By first making themselves irreplaceable to each other in marriage, they have uniquely prepared themselves to stand in for the mother and father of whom the child was deprived.

6.11. ECONOMICS

Q-37 *Some companies argue that unless marriage is redefined to accommodate same-sex couples, they will have difficulty recruiting the best employees to live and work in that state, especially if they are currently living in a state where marriage has already been redefined.*

A It is unconscionable for companies to advocate defining the only institution that unites kids with their moms and dads out of existence for competitive or profit motives. In doing so, they are working against the efforts of the moms and dads working for them, as well as their customers and stockholders who are trying to teach their children about the reality of marriage and human sexuality, and the importance of choosing marriage as the foundation for the next generation.

When companies support the movement to redefine marriage, it also creates a hostile work environment for employees trying to support a culture in which marriage is the foundation of the family—uniting children with their mothers and fathers.

NOTE: This claim is unsupportable. Eight of top ten states for business (*Chief Executive Magazine* CEO survey, 2011, and *Forbes*) have constitutional amendments protecting marriage. Of the ten worst states for business, seven have redefined marriage or have created pseudo-marriage (civil unions) to accommodate same-sex couples.

Corporations have no competency for understanding the human person, the fundamental human rights of a child to be born into a real family with a married mother and father, or the meaning and purpose of marriage.

Q-38 ***Opening marriage to more people will provide more economic activity and jobs due to an increase in weddings by same-sex couples.***

A   This is an argument that is so outrageous it barely justifies a response. It is very shallow to advocate redefining the only institution that unites kids with their moms and dads out of existence for economic gain. This is an example of utilitarianism at its worse—putting pleasure and personal benefits above the good of the person. It is unconscionable to ignore the tragic human cost of the breakdown of marriage and contribute to its further destruction for profit.

Q-39   *Many companies and business leaders endorse and use stockholder funds to promote redefining marriage. That shows acceptance by the establishment.*

A   Giving them the benefit of the doubt, they may not realize that in supporting the redefinition of marriage they are opposing the only public institution that unites kids with their moms and dads. They have aligned themselves with interest groups who effectively argue that there is no public interest in any public institution that promotes the rights of children of knowing and being cared for by their mother and father. That is an outrageous lie and these leaders and companies must be held accountable by the public (customers and stockholders).

6.12.   CIVIL UNIONS AND DOMESTIC PARTNERSHIPS

Q-40   *Wouldn't civil unions or domestic partnerships be a good alternative to redefining marriage? They would recognize the committed relationship between loving same-sex couples and provide the same benefits of marriage without the word.*

A   Out of compassion, many believe that civil unions and domestic partnerships are viable alternatives to redefining marriage to accommodate same-sex couples. They are not. What they create are pseudo-marriages based on a false concept that marriage is merely the public recognition of a committed relationship for the fulfillment of adults. They create the expectation or understanding that these alternatives are equivalent to marriage in value and public interest and become unsatisfying to participants who feel the use of different words to describe the same thing is discriminatory. Experience demonstrates that this opens the door for future law suits and legislation to redefine marriage to accommodate same-sex couples.

Q-41   *Why can't civil unions and domestic partnerships exist side by side with marriage between a man and a woman?*

A   Claims of equality of different but equal "unions" provide the same impediments in the law and to public institutions as if marriage were redefined as merely the public recognition of a committed relationship for the fulfillment of adults. This would likely make it discriminatory and illegal for public and private institutions to promote the unique public interest of men and women marrying before having children. Marriage as equivalent to civil unions and domestic partnerships would have to be taught in schools as being separate and distinct from children and family, or just one alternative if someone wants to have a child. It would become discriminatory for public institutions to have programs that promote marriage as the only institution that unites children with their mothers and fathers and unique value of men and women marrying before having children.[11]

---

11   CDF, *Legal Recognition of Homosexual Unions*, no. 7.

∞⃝

Appendix

Quick Facts About
The Breakdown of Marriage and Family

- <u>41%</u> of children are **born to unmarried mothers** (73% for African Americans)[1]
- <u>71%</u> of **poor families** are **not married**[2]
- **Marriage decreases** the probability a child will live in **poverty** by <u>82%</u>[3]
- **Fatherless or single parent homes** produce children who are
  - <u>2 times</u> more likely to be **arrested for juvenile crime**[4]
  - <u>2 times</u> more likely to be **treated** for emotional and behavioral problems[5]

1   Center for Disease Control, National Vital Statistics, 2009.
2   Robert Rector, "Marriage: America's Greatest Weapon Against Child Poverty," Heritage Foundation, 2010, http://www.heritage.org/research/reports/2010/09/marriage-america-s-greatest-weapon-against-child-poverty.
3   Ibid.
4   Chris Coughlin and Samuel Vuchinich, "Family Experience in Preadolescence and the Development of Male Delinquency," *Journal of Marriage and Family*, vol. 58, no. 2 (1996): 491–501.
5   Deborah A. Dawson, "Family Structure and Children's Health and Well-Being: Data from the 1988 National Health Interview Survey on Child Health," *Journal of Marriage and Family*, vol. 53, no. 3 (August 1991): 573–584.

- **2 times** more likely to be **suspended or expelled** from school[6]
- **33% more likely to drop out of school**[7]
- **3 times** more likely to **end up in jail by age 30**[8]
- Compared to a married mother and father,[9] children living with an unmarried mother
  - and **biological father** are **4 times** more likely to be **sexually, physically or emotionally abused;**
  - and a boyfriend are **11 times** more likely to be **sexually, physically or emotionally abused;**
  - and **biological father** are **3 times** more likely to be **physically, emotionally, or educationally neglected;**
  - and a boyfriend are **6 times** more likely to be **physically, emotionally, or educationally neglected.**

The effects of marriage breakdown on children continue into adulthood.
- **Compared to intact families, children raised by single parents**
  - **are 50%** more likely **to suffer poverty** as adults[10]

---

6 Wendy D. Manning and Kathleen A. Lamb, "Adolescent Well-Being in Cohabiting, Married, and Single-Parent Families," *Journal of Marriage and Family*, vol. 65, no. 4 (2003): 876–893. Data from Add Health study. See also Dawson, "Family Structure and Children's Health and Well-Being: Data from the 1988 National Health Interview Survey on Child Health."

7 Timothy Biblarz and Greg Gottainer, "Family Structure and Children's Success: A Comparison of Widowed and Divorced Single-Mother Families," *Journal of Marriage and Family*, vol. 62 (May 2000): 533–548.

8 Rector, "Marriage," Heritage Foundation.

9 Fourth National Incidence Study of Child Abuse and Neglect, U.S. Dept. Health and Human Services, 2011.

10 Rector, "Marriage," Heritage Foundation.

- **Compared to intact families, girls raised by single parents**
  - **are 2 times** more likely **to have a child** outside of marriage[11]

Attitudes about Marriage Call for Need to Promote the Reality of Marriage

- High school seniors: 56%—OK to be unmarried and have children[12]
- 18- to 39-year-olds: 30%—"Marriage is very important if a couple has children together"[13]
- 18- to 29-year-olds: 44%—Marriage is obsolete[14]

---

11 Ibid.
12 Bradford Wilcox, *State of our Unions, Marriage in America 2009,* data from University of Michigan, http://www.stateofourunions.org/2009/index.php.
13 Gallup Poll, May 2006. http://www.gallup.com/poll/23041/americans-complex-relationship-marriage.aspx.
14 Pew: *The Decline of Marriage and Rise of New Families.*

TO ORDER ADDITIONAL COPIES

Phone: (800) 398- 5470 (M-F, 9-5 ET)
(740) 283-2880
Fax: (740) 283-4011

Email: questions@emmausroad.org

Online: www.emmausroad.org, Amazon,
or your local Catholic bookstores

Mail: Emmaus Road Publishing
827 N. Fourth Street
Steubenville, OH 43952

—————— or ——————

Phone: (415) 651-4171 San Francisco Office
(213) 291 3580 Los Angeles Office
Fax: (415) 738-0421

Email: info@ccgaction.org

Online: www.ccgaction.org

Mail: Catholics for the Common Good
P.O. Box 320038
San Francisco, CA 94132-0038

Bulk Pricing

1-5 copies $5.95 each	21-50 copies $4.46 each
6-20 copies $5.35 each	51-100 copies $3.57 each
101-250 copies $2.98 each	Over 250 copies $2.38 each

What People are saying about
Catholics for the Common Good

"CCGI works cooperatively with the bishops by organizing and supporting the laity in the fulfillment of their unique secular responsibilities in the mission of the Church—working for just social order that coincides with God's plan for creation."

Archbishop George Niederauer
Archdiocese of San Francisco

"Catholics for the Common Good is bringing fresh new insights to the application of authentic Catholic social teaching to messaging and strategy on issues related to sexuality, marriage, and family."

Edward Dolesji,
Executive Director
California Catholic Conference

"CCGI's approach is positive, based on Catholic social teaching and the method of John Paul II. I encourage parishes and individuals within the Diocese of San Diego to learn more about their apostolate. This type of formation and action is essential for promoting the reality of marriage and protecting children and families."

Bishop Robert H. Brom
Diocese of San Diego

Join the movement

. . . a growing community evangelizing the culture for marriage and family.

- *A positive reality-based approach for rebuilding a marriage culture*

- *Training, formation and faith sharing circles of love*

- *Local networks for coordinated action*

- *Speakers bureaus*

- *Seminars and workshops*

- *Community outreach to community organizations and leaders*

For more information go to
standwithchildren.org
or write to
info@ccgaction.org